matariki

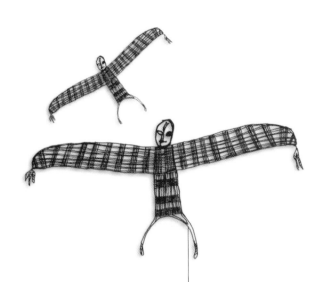

For Oriwa Kurupae Rongo

who celebrates her first

birthday on Matariki 2004

matariki

THE MĀORI NEW YEAR

LIBBY HAKARAIA

RAUPO

A RAUPO BOOK
Published by the Penguin Group
Penguin Group (NZ), 67 Apollo Drive, Rosedale,
North Shore 0632, New Zealand (a division of Pearson New Zealand Ltd)
Penguin Group (USA) Inc., 375 Hudson Street,
New York, New York 10014, USA
Penguin Group (Canada), 90 Eglinton Avenue East, Suite 700, Toronto,
Ontario, M4P 2Y3, Canada (a division of Pearson Penguin Canada Inc.)
Penguin Books Ltd, 80 Strand, London, WC2R 0RL, England
Penguin Ireland, 25 St Stephen's Green,
Dublin 2, Ireland (a division of Penguin Books Ltd)
Penguin Group (Australia), 250 Camberwell Road, Camberwell,
Victoria 3124, Australia (a division of Pearson Australia Group Pty Ltd)
Penguin Books India Pvt Ltd, 11, Community Centre,
Panchsheel Park, New Delhi – 110 017, India
Penguin Books (South Africa) (Pty) Ltd, 24 Sturdee Avenue,
Rosebank, Johannesburg 2196, South Africa

Penguin Books Ltd, Registered Offices: 80 Strand, London, WC2R 0RL, England

Originally published by Reed Publishing (NZ) Ltd, 2004
Reprinted 2005

First published by Penguin Group (NZ), 2008
5 7 9 10 8 6

Copyright © Libby Hakaraia, 2004

Cover and text designed by Sally Fullam
Cover image: Robyn Kahukiwa, *Matariki*, oil on board, 1750 x 1000 mm.
Courtesy of Mokaimarutuna Scott.
The author and the publishers have made every effort to acknowledge
the source of illustrative material included in this book
Printed in China through Asia Pacific Offset

ISBN: 978 0 14 301018 0

A catalogue record for this book is available
from the National Library of New Zealand.

www.penguin.co.nz

CONTENTS

AUTHOR'S NOTE

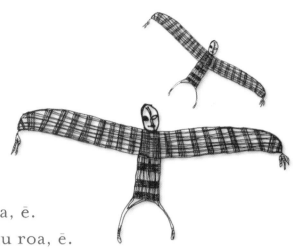

Matariki atua ka eke mai i te rangi e roa, ē.
Whāngainga iho ki te mata o te tau roa, ē.

To Matariki the stars that herald the return of light,
bringing new life, new growth.

I HAVE ALWAYS been fascinated by the night sky. But like most I knew very little about what it contains.

Some years ago I spent 18 months crisscrossing the Atlantic Ocean, crewing on yachts. Most times I would volunteer for the midnight to dawn watch. It allowed me to see an awesome display of stars set against the ink-black sky. On occasion I would lie on the deck and with the motion of the yacht I felt as if the sky wrapped around me and I was a traveller in the heavens. I often thought how people had tried to make 'sense' of the night sky since human life had begun. During recent months I have once again found myself captivated by the night sky while living in the relatively isolated village of Te Tii Mangonui. The absence of street lights and neighbouring houses provides for fantastic displays of the Milky Way and all the stars that spill out around it.

It was a case of serendipity and some gentle cajoling that led to me taking up the opportunity from Reed Publishing to write this book about Matariki.

During my research I have met some inspiring people. I have been able to combine my passion for New Zealand history and traditions with a respect for science and lore.

I hope you enjoy this book . . . and that one day soon we may all light small fires, sing and dance as we welcome Matariki for another year.

Kia ora

LIBBY HAKARAIA

ACKNOWLEDGEMENTS

THE WRITING OF this book would not have been possible without the help of a large number of people.

My thanks firstly to the contributors for their expertise and guidance. To Kay Leather and Richard Hall of the Carter Observatory in Wellington for your patience and encouragement.

My gratitude to science writer Vicki Hyde of Christchurch and to Marilyn Head, editor of *Galaxy Magazine*.

I acknowledge the assistance of the staff at the Museum of New Zealand Te Papa Tongarewa.

Ngā mihi aroha ki a matua Hapimana Rikihana i Ōtautahi. Ngā mihi nui hoki ki a Hekenukumai Busby i te Tai Tokerau.

To the very good people at Reed Publishing for your gentle insistence that I should write this book. Tēnā kōrua Gillian Kootstra kōrua ko Peter Dowling. A special thanks to Sally Fullam for her cover and text design.

To Robyn Kahukiwa for the cover image. Ko te tino ātaahua, whaea.

To my dear friend and guide Henare te Ua my aroha always.

And to Glenn Colquhoun for his unerring support and for providing me with a wonderful place to write.

Ka nui aku mihi ki a koutou.

INTRODUCTION

The fact that the appearance of Pleiades — Matariki — is not now well known is proof of the fact that when old customs die, they die indeed.

SO WROTE BROADCASTER, educationalist and former New Zealand Race Relations Conciliator Harry Dansey in 1967.

Now, almost four decades later, the celebration of Matariki — like so many Māori traditions — is undergoing a renaissance. All around New Zealand a growing number of events are being held to coincide with Matariki's appearance in the dawn sky in the middle of the year.

Matariki is the name given by Māori to a cluster of stars that rises on the northeastern horizon around the end of May each year. This is the constellation familiar to the ancient Greeks and modern astronomers as Pleiades.

The Pleiades star cluster, also known as the Seven Sisters and Messier 45, was celebrated in the ancient world, from Greece to India. We now know the cluster contains hundreds of stars, of which only a handful are commonly visible to the unaided eye.

Māori assigned names to seven of the stars in the Matariki group and waited eagerly for their first rising in the dawn sky each year. This was usually a time of plenty: kūmara and other crops had been stored, birds and fish were abundant. The first moon, usually a week after Matariki was first seen, was celebrated as the Māori New Year — a time of feasting, song and remembering of those who had passed away. Matariki was also looked to as a sign of how plentiful the harvest would be,

the com ng weather, and as a guide for food-gathering and navigation.

Today there are calls for Matariki to be celebrated by all New Zealanders as a national day. Some say this would be more in keeping with the way the seasons of Aotearoa New Zealand were originally measured, as opposed to continuing to follow th calendar and traditions of the northern hemisphere.

Aside from this debate, a growing number of people are taking an interest in the night skies of New Zealand and especially in Matariki. This is in part due to the enthusiasm and teaching abilities of people such as Richard Hall and Kay Leather of the Carter Observatory and the Phoenix Astronomical Society, and the principals behind the newly opened Stonehenge Aotearoa in the Wairarapa (a facility that will help revive Māori astronomical lore and traditions associated with constellations such as Matariki). The Museum of New Zealand Te Papa Tongarewa, city councils and schools have also been observing Matariki.

Astronomy is the oldest of all the sciences. Knowledge of the daily and seasonal movements of the sun, moon and stars were essential to the survival of early communities, including Māori. Perhaps, a century after the 1922 publication of Elsdon Best's important work *Astronomical Knowledge of the Maori*, Matariki will be recognised and celebrated by all New Zealanders. And while Best may be right when he says that much of Māori star lore is now lost, it is possible that interest in Matariki and the research this generates will encourage new generations of Māori and non-Māori to rediscover this ancient knowledge and carry it forward into future centuries.

I haere mai koe i te ao Puanga
I te huihui o Matariki
I a Pareārau, i a Poutū-te-rangi
Ka mutu, e tama, ngā whetū homai kai ki Aotea.

You came hither from the realm of Puanga (Rigel)
From the assembly of Matariki
From Jupiter, and from Poutū-te-rangi
These alone, O child, are the stars which provide food at Aotea.

(The opening lines of a lullaby)

LIBBY HAKARAIA

HOW MATARIKI CAME TO BE

Nā Tāne i toko, ka mawehe Rangi rāua ko Papa,
Nana i tauwehea ai ka heuea te Po, ka heuea te Ao.

By the pushing of Tāne, Ranginui and Papatūānuku were thrust apart,
By him they were separated, and the darkness and light were disengaged.

TE WHĀNAU MĀRAMA

BEFORE EUROPEANS CAME to New Zealand, Māori knew the stars (whetū) and other lights in the night sky as 'Te Whānau Mārama' (the family of light). They had many stories that explained the origins and relationships of Te Whānau Mārama. Some tribes say the members of this whānau are spread throughout 12 different heavens. Ranginui, the Sky Father, occupies the heaven closest to earth. He is the husband of Papatūānuku, the Earth Mother, and their offspring are Te Whānau Mārama.

In some stories, two of their children — Tangotango and Wainui — are said to have created the sun, moon and stars. Other tribal histories have Tangotango pairing with Moe-te-āhuru to produce the sun (Tama-nui-te-rā) and the moon (Marama-i-whanake). Tangotango and Moe-te-āhuru then turned their attentions to making the stars. These stars are the youngest members of Te Whānau Mārama.

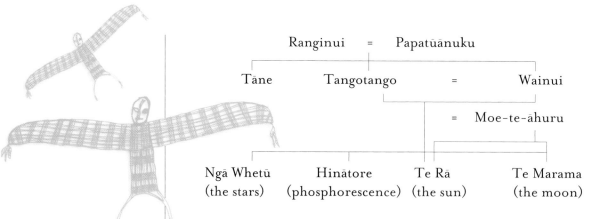

Ranginui = Papatūānuku

Tāne   Tangotango = Wainui

= Moe-te-āhuru

Ngā Whetū (the stars)   Hinātore (phosphorescence)   Te Rā (the sun)   Te Marama (the moon)

In another story it was Uru-te-ngangana, a third son of Ranginui and Papatūānuku, who fathered the sun, moon and stars. His first wife, Hine-te-āhuru, bore him the sun and the moon, and his second wife, Hine-tūrama, the stars.

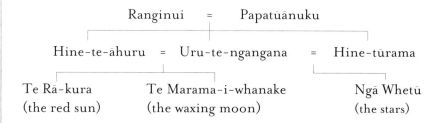

Ranginui = Papatūānuku

Hine-te-āhuru = Uru-te-ngangana = Hine-tūrama

Te Rā-kura (the red sun)   Te Marama-i-whanake (the waxing moon)   Ngā Whetū (the stars)

One of the most important children of Ranginui and Papatūānuku is Tāne. Tāne was responsible for separating his parents so that the world as we know it could exist. Tāne's role as the creator of the night skies is told in a number of stories.

In one version Tāne is said to have visited his brother Tangotango to congratulate him on the brilliance of his children — the sun, moon and stars. Tāne asked Tangotango if he could take these bright offspring to provide light between their separated parents, Ranginui and Papatūānuku. But Tangotango was unsure, allowing only Hinātore (phosphorescent light) to go. Tāne placed Hīnātore against Ranginui. A sliver of light altered the darkness.

Tāne next asked for and received the stars, and a dim light soon spread from Ranginui. After acquiring the moon from Tangotango, the light grew stronger. Finally, Tāne asked for and received Tama-nui-te-rā, the sun. Light entered the

OPPOSITE PAGE: Summer evening sky from Aotearoa looking north. Matariki 'The Food Bringer' (Pleiades star cluster) is on the edge of the Milky Way (lower left). Due north, above and to the right of Matariki, is Tautoru 'The Birdsnare' (constellation of Orion). Above Tautoru is the Tui 'The Guardian of the Months'. To the right is Whakaahu (Gemini) which heralds the spring when it rises just before the sun.
Richard Hall and Kay Leather

LIBBY HAKARAIA

space between Ranginui and Papatūānuku, and Te Ao Mārama — the world of light — was created.

Tāne is said to have placed the stars on Ranginui's head, body and limbs, the moon on his stomach and the sun on his chest. As a result Ranginui's face and body were bathed in light while his mokopuna (grandchildren) danced on his body.

It was not long before problems began to appear in Te Ao Mārama. The heat from the sun was scorching Papatūānuku, and Ranginui was also finding the warmth and intensity from the stars on his head too much. Tāne asked Te Ikaroa (the Milky Way) to space out the various courses of the stars and the moon so that his parents could get some sleep. The night then became the domain of the moon, the stars and the Milky Way.

The pathways that Te Whānau Mārama travelled to provide light for Ranginui can be traced in the pattern of stars in our night sky. Some say baskets were used to ferry them from far-off Maunganui and bring them to Tāne so he could place them on his father's body. The sun was put in one basket, the moon in another and the stars in a basket called Te Ikaroa.

Others say a canoe was used to transport Te Whānau Mārama. This canoe belonged to Tama-rereti and is still seen in the heavens. It is known as Te Waka o Tama-rereti or the Tail of the Scorpion.

Ka mārama koe ki te kete a Tāne
I mauria atu nei hei tohu mō tōna matua
Tātaitia rā, tāwhaia i runga rā
Ki Autahi ē, ki a Puanga rāia
Ki a Takurua rā
Ringia i te kete ko Te Ika-o-te-rangi
Ka nako i runga nei.

Be clear as to the receptacle of Tāne
Conveyed by him as a token for his parent.
Arranged and dotted on high
Were Canopus, Rigel and Sirius.
The Milky Way was poured out from the receptacle
And now adorns the firmament.

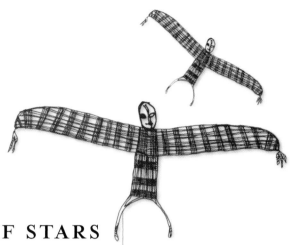

MATARIKI — A CLUSTER OF STARS

Mata-ariki, the eyes of god

LEFT: Matariki.
Adapted from an image
of the Pleiades in the
northern hemisphere
(rotated 180°).
*© Jerry Lodriguss/
www.astropix.com*

MATARIKI IS SAID to be one of the offspring of Ranginui and Papatūānuku. Some tribes refer to him as a male and the younger brother of Tangotango. However, the group is most often looked upon as a female deity. The name Matariki comes from the Māori words mata, eyes, and ariki, god.

Early European astronomers in New Zealand were intrigued that Māori could make out seven stars with the naked eye, when they could see only five. Many years later when telescopes were trained on the cluster, it was confirmed that there were in fact seven major stars in this constellation.

Many people say that Matariki is the name given to the cluster of seven stars. However, others believe Matariki to be the name of the largest star, with the other six stars in the cluster being her sisters. Their names are included in this account recorded by Elsdon Best in 1890: 'Pio, of Ngati-Awa, gave the names of the six prominent stars of the group as Tupua-nuku, Tupua-rangi, Waiti, Waita, Waipuna-a-rangi and Ururangi'.

WHERE MATARIKI CAN BE FOUND

Many a night I saw the Pleiades, rising thro' the mellow shade,
　　Glitter like a swarm of fireflies tangled in a silver braid.

Alfred Lord Tennyson

According to astronomers, Matariki is a cluster of stars situated in the constellation Taurus. Roughly 400 light years from Earth, it is one of the most visible collections of stars in the night sky. There are nearly 500 stars in the group but only a handful are visible without a telescope.

Depending on where you live in Aotearoa New Zealand, Matariki should be visible around the end of May, rising over the northeastern horizon, at a point near where the sun rises.

LIBBY HAKARAIA

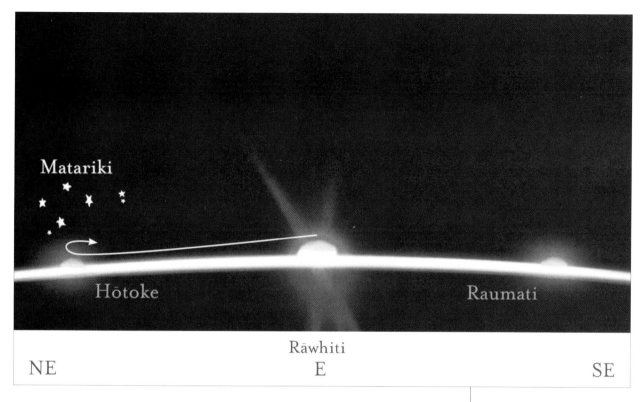

NE	Rāwhiti E	SE

The illustration (above) shows the movement of the sunrise across the horizon over the year. In Raumati (summer) the sun rises in the southeast. As the year progresses the sun moves along the eastern horizon. Once it passes the shortest day of Hōtoke (winter) and reaches the northeastern end of the horizon Matariki appears and the sun turns and begins travelling south again.

ABOVE: Matariki rising at dawn. *Adapted from* Matariki: Te Whetu o Tē Tau, *Te Taura Whiri i te Reo Maori*

MAHI WHAI —
HAPIMANA'S STORY

ABOVE: Hapimana Rikihana (Te Arawa) demonstrates the art of mahi whai (Māori string patterns). The pattern is the separation of Ranginui and Papatūānuku.

IN PRE-PĀKEHĀ times mahi whai (Māori string patterns) were used to illustrate and enhance kōrero and pakiwaitara (stories). Hapimana Rikihana grew up in Rotorua in the Māori village, Te Puna.

I went to Whakarewarewa Primary School where we were encouraged to speak te reo Māori and to know our tikanga. So we knew about Matariki and although we didn't celebrate it, I know that my kuia and some of the old people, the pakeke, still practised the old ways. This is where I began learning mahi whai. It's almost a dead art but in the old days men and women, old and young, performed it. It was an essential part of mahi toi in those days. It was on a par with mahi tāniko, kōwhaiwhai, whatu kākahu and those things. It was not considered as string games just for children. They were not in the days of our old people but part of the depth of our tikanga Māori. All my life I have been a teacher and I have used mahi whai to keep alive the stories of our many whetū.

Today, the art of mahi whai remains relevant not only to Matariki but also to other whetū. I believe it is a great teaching tool and could revive a deep interest in tātai arorangi (astronomy) and lead us back to celebrating Matariki as our old people did.

LEFT: Hapimana Rikihana creates the mahi whai for Matariki. Note the seven diamonds in the pattern.

RIGHT: Kōpū, Tāwera: Venus, the Evening Star.

Māori used mahi whai to recreate the patterns they saw in the night sky. Through the patterns, the stories and cosmology were remembered and Māori star lore and knowledge were passed on.

WHY MATARIKI WAS IMPORTANT

Te huihui o Matariki
        The gathering of Matariki

THE NIGHT SKY was inspiring to pre-European Māori. It was vast and unfathomable, but they had ways of making sense of it and learnt to read it and use its clues to help them in their daily lives. It also was the basis of their principal method of measuring time and ordering the environment around them. The sun, moon and stars all played a part in each of the months of the Māori calendar and most Māori knew how to read the skies with the same ease that people read a wristwatch today.

The gathering and cultivation of food were central to pre-European Māori. Knowing when to plant and harvest crops was vital to survival. One of the most obvious reasons that Matariki was important to the Māori of this time was that its rising provided a sign to begin preparing the soil for the planting of crops. It also became a marker for the beginning of the new year itself, associated with people's need to celebrate their joys, look forward to better days and reflect on the loss of loved ones during the year that had passed.

Matariki was also important to this people of a sea-going culture because it provided travellers with a reference point for navigation.

Because of these roles, it is not surprising that Matariki was seen, in part, as an oracle — an entity that could explain and order the unexplained. It was studied for clues about the size of future crops and the patterns of weather.

20

Matariki ahunga nui — Matariki of abundant food

Matariki tāpuapua — Matariki of many pools

Matariki hunga nui — Matariki widely followed

Matariki kanohi iti — Matariki of small eyes

These proverbs hint at the many different ways in which Matariki was important to Māori. Matariki was a pointer to collecting food. It appeared in winter in New Zealand and so was associated with pools of water on the ground. It gathered people together, and it appeared as small eyes in the sky at night.

LEFT: Te Rā, the sun, rises over the hills bringing life and fertility to Papatūānuku (the Earth Mother). *Kay Leather*

THE MĀORI CALENDAR
AND CROP GROWING

Hauhake tū, ka tō Matariki.

Lifting of the crops begins when Matariki sets.

WHEN MĀORI CAME to Aotearoa they found it to be colder than their Polynesian homelands. The foods they were accustomed to could not be grown without considerable effort. To take advantage of the differently timed growing season, Māori reordered their yearly calendar. The planting of crops began not with the rising of Matariki at sunset in November, as it does in other Polynesian cultures, but in June when Matariki is seen in Aotearoa in the dawn sky.

The Māori year centred on crop growing. It was labour-intensive work. For 10 months of the year most members of the tribe would be cultivating, planting, tending and harvesting their crops.

The Māori months were measured by the phases of the moon, by the path of the sun in its annual course and by the stars. One night in autumn, Matariki would set. Through the autumn, the rising sun would travel along the eastern horizon, appearing further and further north until the shortest day of the year in winter, when it reached the point where Matariki would rise again. From that point the sun would turn and begin travelling on its southward journey.

As the sunrise travelled north, lookouts would scan the dawn sky for the rise of the star Whānui (Vega), which occurred about two months before the next rising of Matariki. As soon as Whānui was seen, the village would be woken and

LIBBY HAKARAIA

ABOVE: Judy Rangi (Turanga/ Rongowhakaata) with her grandfather Wiremu Tamihana Rangi.

JUDY'S STORY

Judy Rangi was brought up by her grandparents in Gisborne. She recalls hearing her grandparents and her elder aunties and uncles discussing Matariki events. On the morning of the appearance of Matariki, Judy says she would be woken and taken outside to the family's garden.

I remember having to get up and plant watermelon and sugar cane. The sun would be just coming up and I would be standing over the hole, planting. Planting watermelon seeds. My grandparents told me it had to be done by a young person and that would be about the only time I got in the garden. I didn't have to weed it and I wasn't allowed in the garden because I would pull up the plants. Except for Matariki. But I didn't know the stories associated with Matariki back then, as a child. It was only many years later that I heard people talking about Matariki again and about planting and I thought my grandparents used to like to observe its rising.

ABOVE: Aunty Huia
Heihei's kūmara garden,
Te Tii Mangonui,
Northland.

the tohunga would study a kūmara dug from the soil to decide whether harvesting could begin. This was in the month known as Ngahuru (March–April). Ngahuru was also the time when the star Poutū-te-rangi (which refers to the stars Altair or Antares) was seen, and many tribes now refer to the tenth month by the name of this star.

Once the crops had been harvested the tribes would turn their attention to other activities, including fishing and birding, socialising or warfare. Therefore, the two months between the harvest and new planting were considered the 'time off' months. This is why the Māori calendar has been spoken of as being 10 months plus two.

Trees and medicinal plants were also planted at Matariki.

LIBBY HAKARAIA

MATARIKI AND THE GATHERING OF BIRDS AND FISHES

Ka rere a Matariki, ka wera te hinu.
>When Matariki rises, the fat is heated.

THE MAIN SEASON for gathering birds in pre-European Aotearoa began about May and lasted for approximately three months. This was particularly so for tribes who had crops to plant and tend. However, tribes whose main food source was birds would hunt for a longer period.

This proverb indicates that Matariki was the start of the bird-preserving activities or huahua manu:

Ka kitea a Matariki a kua maoka te hinu —
>Once Matariki is seen then the preserved flesh is obtained

Huahua was the name given to the preserving and potting of birds in their own fat. Bird catchers began collecting their prey up to a fortnight before Matariki was due to appear. A team of women would then prepare the birds for preserving. Once the birds had been plucked, cleaned and boned they would be

RIGHT: The kereru (New Zealand wood pigeon) was widely hunted by Māori. It was one of the main birds preserved by the huahua method. Nowadays it is protected.
Geoff Moon

packed in baskets. These baskets were left in water until Matariki was seen rising and the ahi mātiti could begin.

The ahi mātiti was the roasting of the birds over a clean fire of either charcoal or glowing hardwood embers that emitted no smoke. The birds were cooked on racks and the fat that dripped from them was collected in a trough. The roasted birds were placed in a vessel such as a gourd, the fat poured over them and the vessel sealed. The gourd was decorated with feathers, and carved legs made of bone or wood were added.

The huahua manu was a most desirable dish. During the Matariki celebrations and throughout the year at special feasts huahua manu would be presented to honoured guests. A good season saw many gourds of huahua manu stored for the coming year.

LIBBY HAKARAIA

The appearance of Matariki also had a role to play in fishing, as this proverb relates:

Ka kitea a Matariki, ka rere te korokoro
When Matariki is seen, the korokoro (lamprey) migrate.

It was said that when Matariki rose, fish such as the moki and the korokoro could be caught. River tribes fished for korokoro with large nets. What was caught was eaten during the Matariki celebrations or traded for other foods in short supply. Fishermen also dried their catches for the lean winter months ahead.

LEFT: Tāmure (snapper) are fat and plentiful in Hōtoke (winter) in Te Tii Mangonui.

THE MĀORI NEW YEAR
— TE TAU HOU

Ngā kai a Matariki, nāna i ao ake ki runga.

The foods of Matariki, by her brought forth.

IT WAS THE first moon after the rising of Matariki that was widely viewed as the start of the Māori year. It was a time of plenty; the crops had been stored and tribes were engaged in fishing and birding.

According to Hapimana Rikihana:

> The start of the New Year varies in each area. For an area next to the tātahi [sea] they would see Matariki differently than say a settlement in the bush area or in a farming area. I would go ask a pakeke or kaumātua in different areas what they know. Elsdon Best is a good starting point but ultimately I think it is what a community thinks and does or has done in the past, and if communities are lucky enough to have these old people still alive then they should be looked after and resourced for the knowledge that they may have. But Matariki is definitely an important event in the Māori year or the maramataka Māori.

In times past, feasting and universal joy marked the arrival of Matariki. Parties of women faced the star group and greeted it with song and dance. However, it may have been that Matariki was observed in two parts. The first sighting of Matariki

LIBBY HAKARAIA

was celebrated with karakia, laments, songs of joy and dancing. But it was the time of the first moon after the initial rising of the star cluster that was associated with feasting. Few written accounts can be found regarding the celebrations, but John White records the following:

> The tapu period of the year was when Matariki appeared above the horizon in the morning. That was the occasion on which our elders of former times held festivals when the people rejoiced and women danced and sang for joy as they looked on Matariki.

For some Māori, notably Ngāpuhi in Northland and those living in the Chatham Islands, the New Year commenced with the rising of Rigel. Rigel is a star in the constellation of Orion and is known to Māori as Puanga.

Great celebrations were held when Matariki was first seen.
It was described as: 'a notable event in Māori-land . . .
greeted in two ways — by laments for those who had died recently,
and by women with singing and posture dances'.

Elsdon Best

In an interview recorded by Elsdon Best in the early 1900s, an elder remarked that 'The task of Puanga is to strive with Matariki that he may gain possession of the year.'

For Ngāpuhi and some Ngāi Tahu tribes the helical rising of Puanga [when the star rises just before the sun] was watched for intently, rising just minutes before Matariki. These tribes welcomed Puanga with chanting and offerings of tapu food. Puanga, like Matariki, was seen as a 'food bringer'.

Harry Dansey writes of a note he received in 1957 from the late Rangihuna Pirie of South Taranaki. The old man was then in his seventies and talked of his childhood in the late 1880s or 1890s, and of being taken by his grandparents to watch for Matariki. Rangihuna said that sometimes the old people might wait up for several nights awaiting the appearance of the stars of Matariki. When they did, the people would greet the stars with weeping and recounting of the names of those who had died in the past year. A small hāngī was prepared, and when it was uncovered:

'. . . the scent of the food would rise and strengthen the stars, for they were weak and cold'.

LIBBY HAKARAIA

Today at tangihanga (funerals), speakers still use this proverb:

Haere atu rā, e koro,
ki te paepae o Matariki,
o Rehua.
Haere atu rā.

Farewell, old man,
go to the threshold of Matariki,
of Rehua.
Farewell.

The following lament was written when Matariki was still a vital part of Māori life:

Tirohia atu nei; ka whetūrangitia
Matariki, te whitu o te tau
E whakamoe mai rā, he homai ana rongo
Kia kōmai atu au, ka mate nei au
I te matapōuri, i te matapōrehu
O roto i a au.

Look away here, Matariki is appearing in the sky
The seven stars of the New Year,
Twinkling there giving their tidings that make me rejoice,
I am full of sorrow, full of sadness within.

Mere Reweti Taingunguru (Te Whānau-a-Apanui) refers to Matariki in a lament on the death of her husband, who was killed after leaving her at daybreak:

Tērā Matariki huihui ana mai.
Ka ngaro rā, ē, te whetū kukume ata.

Behold Matariki is gathered above.
Lost, alas, is the star that hauls forth the dawn.

TOHUNGA TĀTAI ARORANGI

Tēnā ngā kanohi kua tikona e Matariki.

Those are the eyes that have been taken by Matariki.

Applied to a person who is wakeful at night.

MĀORI, LIKE MANY ancient people, looked to the heavens for guidance in their daily lives. They attributed many things to the stars, revering them as gods who were both good and bad, kind and harsh. It was the job of the tohunga (a priest or expert), skilled in the lore of tātai arorangi (the direction of the stars), to convey the deeper knowledge and lore of the domain of Ranginui. The tohunga was schooled in the names of the stars and planets and their associated stories. The tribespeople believed that he could communicate with the gods who lived in the heavens and could pass on messages, teachings or warnings of disasters. The tohunga was called upon by the tribe to explain daily and seasonal weather patterns, including foretelling whether the coming harvest was going to be good. He was also called upon to ascribe meanings to, and create stories about, newborn children as well as people who had passed on. The tohunga's expertise in reading the weather was especially sought by fishermen and the captains of voyaging waka. Oral traditions tell us there were tohunga tātai arorangi on all the waka that migrated to Aotearoa.

Another role of the tohunga tātai arorangi was to keep the village safe by providing warnings about attacks by other tribes. The tohunga would spend his

LIBBY HAKARAIA

nights scanning the sky for signs and portents that he could decipher for the chief and the tribe. He would study the phases of the moon to be sure of the timing of a new moon, when the night would be very dark. War parties often carried out raids at this time. The tohunga was relied on both to forewarn against attacks and, conversely, to provide the best time to launch an assault.

> Some very curious auguries and omens were derived from the stars, and this is one reason why certain persons closely and persistently scanned them. A star in a position close to the moon excited much interest, the omen depending upon its position. If it is 'biting' — that is, near — the mata o hoturoa, or cusp of the crescent moon, it betokens the approach of an enemy force. Such omens often caused natives to take careful precautions against being surprised.
>
> *Elsdon Best*

The time before and just after Matariki, when many people of the tribe were away from their fortified villages fishing and bird-hunting, was also the time when war parties were sent out to exact utu (vengeance) for past transgressions or to raid storehouses. It was therefore a time for the tohunga to be especially watchful of the night sky.

ABOVE: A tohunga.
Drawing from W. Dittmer,
Te Tohunga *(1907)*

MATARIKI THE SIGNALLER

Matariki atua ka eke mai i te rangi e roa, ē.
Whāngainga iho ki te mata o te tau e roa, ē.

Divine Matariki come forth from the far-off heaven,
bestow the first fruits of the year upon us.

MĀORI SAW MATARIKI not only as the 'bringer of foods' but also as a signaller as to whether the year ahead would be bountiful. It was widely believed that the first sighting of Matariki, the helical rising, was the best time to 'read' the group as to what lay ahead in the coming year.

If the stars of Matariki appeared widely spaced then it would be a warm season in which food would be plentiful. If they were close together and appeared hazy or seemed to quiver or move, this spelt a time of bitter weather and lean pickings.

The portent of things is always related to the dawn sky and there is an almost universal belief that there is a cycle of life, death and resurrection. If you notice the stars are moving on a night-by-night basis they are moving closer and closer to the sun and disappear from view so you will see Matariki towards the end of May heading closer and closer towards the Western horizon heading towards the sun and then it disappears. Māori used to believe they were consumed by the sun and reborn from the sun and so a keen watch was kept for the rising of the star just before the sun in the twilight of a morning sky.

Richard Hall, astronomer, Carter Observatory, Wellington

LIBBY HAKARAIA

Matariki could also be a deliverer of omens. Riwai Te Hiwinui Tawhiri of Ngāti Porou claims that as a boy he witnessed a ceremony that involved seeking an omen before going whaling. The ceremony consisted of elders preparing in the hours before dawn a hāngī of a small amount of food (usually kūmara). They would light the hāngī and then wait for the appearance of Matariki before uncovering the hāngī. If the food was well cooked, it was a successful omen and the whaling would go well; if the food was not cooked, it was a warning not to go ahead with the expedition. Riwai said that those who disobeyed very often met with an accident. This ceremony was said to take place at Otaruia, the principal whaling station between Gisborne and Reporua.

Later on in the Māori lunar year, Matariki was also sought as a protector:

> The stars that are guides for the seasons are eternal, and are ever flashing in the heavens. Our forbears consulted those sign-giving stars in connection with the planting of the kumara crop. The principal stars so relied on were Rigel, the Pleiades, Orion's Belt (Tautoru) and Whakahu (Castor). According to the manner of their rising, the crops would be planted early or late. I have spoken of these stars as a token of regard for the beings who directed our ancestors and elders, now lost to this world.
>
> *Tribal elder, in John White,* The Ancient History of the Maori

In Whiringa-ā-rangi (the sixth lunar month) the kūmara, the most important and sacred crop of ancient Māori, was planted. When it sprouted it was necessary to ask for the protection of Matariki so that the crop would grow well.

The tribe would conduct a dawn ceremony to invoke the help and protection of Matariki over its crops. The ceremony would involve the chanting of karakia while a selected food was held in the hand. This food then became a kai popoa, or sacred offering, to Matariki and would either be placed on a stick that rested in the ground near where the ceremony had taken place or be placed in, or suspended from, an adjacent tree.

LIBBY HAKARAIA

MATARIKI —
ITS ROLE IN NAVIGATION

When setting out on a voyage, some particular star or constellation
was selected as their guide during the night . . .
The Pleiades were a favourite guiding star with these sailors . . .

Elsdon Best, Polynesian Voyages

MATARIKI WAS AN important beacon for the crews of Polynesian voyaging waka. Elsdon Best includes Matariki among a number of stars seen as important to the journey of the migrating *Takitimu* waka to Aotearoa.

Aboard all ocean-going waka, there would have been expert astronomers — tohunga tātai arorangi — who constantly scanned the sky and discovered a 'sea map' to allow a course to be sailed.

By familiarising themselves with the movements of various stars, the tohunga would order that the prow of the waka be pointed at a particular star on the horizon. A stern star might also be lined up, and there were marked points along the length of the waka which could be cross-checked to ensure the waka was sailing as true a direction as possible.

During the day the steersmen would note the sun, wind and sea conditions and continue to point the prow at where the star would appear in the evening.

Many voyages would begin in the early evening. As the prow star moved higher in the sky another star on the horizon would be chosen and new bearings taken.

HEKENUKUMAI'S STORY

LEFT: Hekenukumai Busby,
Reef Point, Karikari Peninsula,
Northland. *Te Aurere Collection*

ALTHOUGH MUCH OF this knowledge is now lost, Hekenukumai (Hector) Busby has spent the past 30 years reviving the Maori lore of ocean-going waka.

I really started off after we relaunched *Ngā Toki Matawhaorua* in 1973. I was hooked. I did not know much about the stars then. I used to do studies. There were a lot of things I tried to solve. When I read the Takitimu book and it said they used Atutahi (Canopus) and the sun . . . I couldn't understand because the sun was setting at 20° south and Atutahi was sitting on about 53° south. But I couldn't rest . . . I was trying to solve it and all of a sudden it just came to me . . . Sure enough I got the chart and I started from Rarotonga. I actually went in a straight line . . . then I cut down on the angle of Atutahi and . . . found it hit right on East Cape. By day they went towards the sun and by night by Atutahi.

We don't use Matariki because it's often too high in the sky at the time of year that we are crossing oceans. But in 1995 I saw it rise and I will never forget it. We were sailing from Hawaii to Rarotonga and had left on the first of June. Matariki rose on the morning of the eleventh of June that year and it was right there beside us.

I like to see it myself when it rises
    and I feel happy if it is a good year for sailing.
        That is the connection now, with Matariki and voyaging.

Hekenukumai Busby

We were in the northern hemisphere and the stars were up on their side. And when they came up that morning they were beautiful and so bright. And we did have a very good year.

Around the middle of May it [Matariki] disappears. My grandmother would warn us that Matariki was going to dive, kua ruku a Matariki. She would say Matariki has dived and would cause currents that would stir up the seabed that loosened off the seaweed. The next morning, at dawn, she made sure we were all up so that we could collect the agar seaweed. We would be down the beach at dawn on our horses. Reef Point, Parapara was the place. There would be camps out at Reef Point and they are still out there today. They still collect the seaweed and sell it. It's used to make iodine and stuff out of it.

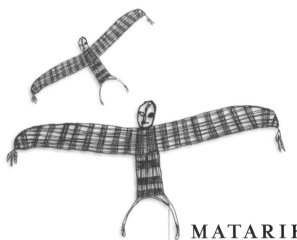

MATARIKI AROUND THE WORLD

Matariki hunga nui.
Matariki has many admirers.

MATARIKI HAD FOUND fame in many cultures well before Māori reached Aotearoa. One of the most famous ancient civilisations, that of ancient Greece, had a number of myths connected with the star cluster that was named Pleiades. The best known of these myths is that the Pleiades are the seven daughters of Pleione and Atlas. Their names were Electra, Maia, Taygete, Alcyone, Celaeno, Sterope and Merope.

One story has the sisters being chased by the hunter Orion who was in love with them. He chased them until the gods intervened and carried them to safety. The sisters were changed into doves and then into stars. According to this legend, Orion is still pursuing them to this day.

> If you go to Greece and go to those temples at the Acropolis they are pointed at the rising of Pleiades. They don't point there now but they did 5000 years ago when they were built. They were at the vernal equinox and that slowly changes. The vernal equinox was the beginning of the year for most of the ancient world.
>
> *Richard Hall*

The Greek derivation of Pleiades may be based on *plen*, 'to sail', making Pleione 'sailing queen' and her daughters 'sailing ones'. In ancient Greece the cluster's

LIBBY HAKARAIA

conjunction with the sun in spring and opposition to it in fall marked the start and end of the summer sailing season, respectively. Or Pleiades may be based on *pleo*, 'full', of which the plural is 'many', an appropriate base for the name of a star cluster.

In the texts of ancient Dravidian India, there are a number of references to the Matariki star cluster. Its stars were revered as the Seven Mothers of the World, one of whom was Kali, and the Seven Priestesses, who made judgement on humankind. An ancient calendar also honoured Matariki during the time now known as November. It was then known as Kartica, the Dravidian word for the Pleiades. Today, in India, the Pleiades are known as the Six Nurses.

In other ancient cultures, there were traditions similar to the Māori practice of offering laments to Matariki.

The Celts marked the appearance of Pleiades with a festival called Beltane, which included dances and songs on the theme of death and resurrection. Bonfires were an important part of the festival. In older times, human sacrifices were made to ensure a fertile season for crops.

In Ireland and throughout northern Europe, there was an All Souls Day tradition of offering prayers for the dead in the direction of Matariki. These

BELOW: The World Rally Car, Subaru Impreza, 2004. *Subaru World Rally Team*

included speaking the names of the Seven Hathors (Matariki), for the souls to begin their 'journey to the paradise in the distant stars'.

In Japan, Matariki is called Subaru, meaning 'gathered together'. Today one of the world's most popular vehicles carries a logo that is a stylised symbol of Matariki.

The Aztec called Matariki Tianquiztl, meaning 'marketplace' or 'gathering place'.

In Egypt, the stars of Matariki are called Chu and are said to represent the 'divine mother and lady of heaven', the Goddess Net or Neith.

In Hebrew, the stars are Kimah, which means 'a cluster'. Kimah is also the word used in some parts of China where mention of the star group first appeared in Chinese texts dated around 2357BC. The Chinese also refer to them as the Blossom Stars and Flower Stars.

In Australia, the Pitjantjatjara tribe knows Matariki as kungkarungkara, the Ancestral Women, while further south the Adnyamathanha people know the stars as Makara, the wives of the stars in the constellation Orion.

The people of the Inca culture called Matariki Little Mothers, or the Seed Scatterer. Festivals were held to celebrate its reappearance in the sky. The Earth was called Paca-Mama, or Earth Mother.

In North America, the Cheyenne Indians tell the Dog Husband story, in which the mother and her children travel to the sky to become the Matariki constellation.

In South Africa, the name Khuseti was used by the Khoikhoi for Matariki. The tribespeople viewed them as the stars of rain, or rain bearers. But in Peru they were called Verano meaning 'dry season'. This was possibly because Matariki appears at the summer solstice during Peru's dry season.

Hindu people called them the Flames of Agni (who was the god of fire in its beneficent form) and considered Matariki to be the wet nurses for Kumara, the god of war.

The Romans knew the cluster as the Bunch of Grapes and the Spring Virgins while the old English, German, Russian, Czech and Hungarian peoples referred to them as the Hen and Chicks.

In Africa, Matariki designates the beginning of the agricultural year.

LIBBY HAKARAIA

MATARIKI IN THE PACIFIC

Pleiades is still celebrated in parts of the Pacific. For most of the peoples of the Pacific, the New Year begins when the cluster rises above the horizon, towards the end of their calendar year.

In Samoa, Matariki is known as Mata-ali'i as well as Mata-ariki. The appearance of the constellation was associated with month-long festivals involving singing, dancing and the blowing of shell trumpets.

An old Hawaiian myth talks of a male constellation named Makali'i — the little eyes. Makali'i is spoken of as a storer of food. According to Elsdon Best, the constellation 'was used in traditional Hawaiian canoe navigation and its appearance was accompanied by a festival of feasting, games, dances and sham fights'. The week-long festival was marked by the chief or ali'i travelling anticlockwise around the islands. By doing this he removed the kapu (tapu) and for the week of the festival there were no rules. After the period of no-rules, the ali'i would then travel clockwise around the islands, thereby restoring kapu and his rule of the country.

In the Cook Islands, the New Year began when Matariki rose just after sunset in December. The Rev. W.W. Gill writes in *Myths and Songs from the South Pacific*: 'Hence the idolatrous worship paid to this beautiful cluster of stars in many of the South Sea Islands'.

At Tahiti Matariki is called Matariíi.

MATARIKI TODAY

E kitea a Matariki i te rāwhiti i te atapō.
Matariki is seen to rise before dawn.

ABOVE: Kay Leather and Richard Hall, astronomers, Carter Observatory, Wellington.

RESEARCH ASTRONOMERS Richard Hall and Kay Leather are at the Carter Observatory in Wellington. Every year they hold public talks about Matariki at the observatory and at places such as Te Papa Tongarewa and in schools and libraries.

Through her ancestral links with Te Aitanga-a-Māhaki of the East Coast, Kay has been researching Māori star lore and includes much of the Māori perspective into her teaching.

You talk to some tribes about Matariki rising but for other tribes it may be Puanga rising so you have to be careful, otherwise you upset that group there. What we try to do is find the underlying thing. You start to see things up there that they saw and the culture, instead of being words, goes back to being what it was. A lot of this knowledge is vested with people who are very old and when they are gone then the knowledge is gone with them.

LIBBY HAKARAIA

Richard Hall and Kay Leather are experts at finding Matariki with the naked eye. If you are unsure how to find the group, contact your local observatory to find out when and where it is due to make its next appearance.

If you see them in a dawn sky when the sky is blue it's almost as if you know they are there — every now and again you see this sparkle coming out of the blue. Today most people wouldn't even notice that but someone who was familiar with the night sky years ago would have seen them. They are tiny little dots. They are noticeable. They are like tiny little diamonds. That's why for some tribes it is Puanga [that is associated with the new year] because it's brighter and bigger and rises at the same time — 30 minutes before Matariki on the horizon.

Richard Hall says:

The average person can see seven but someone with good eyesight can see nine. But there are actually about 400 of them and even more. They have a bluish colour because they are very young hot stars so in the night sky they look very beautiful. Each day after their first appearance they rise four minutes earlier and will be easier to make out because the sky will be slightly darker.

TE PAPA TONGAREWA —
MUSEUM OF NEW ZEALAND

Since the early 1990s staff at Te Papa Tongarewa in Wellington have been active in observing Matariki. Each year the museum publishes a calendar that shows treasures from the Māori collection alongside the Māori names for the days, months, stars and lunar cycles.

BELOW: Dion Pieta and Tamahou Temara playing traditional Māori instruments at the Te Papa Tongarewa Matariki celebrations, 2003.

LIBBY HAKARAIA

In more recent years Te Papa has expanded its commemorations to a month-long series of activities, performances and exhibitions on the theme of Matariki. Arapata Hakiwai (Ngāti Kahungunu, Rongowhakaata) is the director of Mātauranga Māori at Te Papa:

> It has taken a while to grow Matariki events at Te Papa but what better way to commemorate this special time of year for all New Zealanders but by connecting with the taonga that we have here. Not only are we celebrating the Māori New Year but significant cycles in a contemporary way.

ABOVE: Singer Toni Huata (centre) and dancers perform during Matariki festival, Te Papa Tongarewa 2003.

Every year we try and give it a different theme. We have lectures given by people from around the country who share star lore, navigation, songs, etc. People like Pou Temara who spoke of the stars with regards to rituals and karakia. Others have spoken about star lore in mōteatea, waka navigation, Māori astronomers and non-Māori astronomers. One year we looked at notions of time and space — geological time, earth time, different clocks — just to give people a sense of the connections. We celebrate our connection with this land and our identity — and this is an occasion when many New Zealanders like to come and celebrate.

If you wish to be part of the dawn ceremony at Te Papa Tongarewa to mark Matariki, call the museum for details, or check out the website at www.tepapa.govt.nz.

RIGHT: Tom Ward playing a flute at the Matariki Festival. Matariki continues to grow at Te Papa and attract interest from New Zealanders and international visitors alike.

LIBBY HAKARAIA

MATARIKI AS A NATIONAL HOLIDAY

In recent years there have been calls for the Matariki New Year to become a national holiday. Supporters see it as a day of celebration unique to all New Zealanders and an opportunity to create a tradition that is culturally distinct from colonial England. However, for astronomers, the task of setting a day poses problems because New Zealand is on a solar calendar, while old-time Māori used a lunar calendar. This means that the actual time of the New Year floats back and forth depending on when the tohunga note the appearance of Matariki.

SOME WAYS TO CELEBRATE MATARIKI

There are many ways to celebrate the dawn appearance of Matariki today. Local iwi, schools, councils and public institutions may be running programmes so check your local paper.

You may wish to mark the occasion with your family by getting up at dawn and having a small bonfire and picnic. Encourage your children to read and share stories about Matariki. You may wish to reflect on the year that has passed and set goals for the year ahead.

Building and flying your own kite is one way to celebrate Matariki. Pre-European Maori and many other Polynesian cultures flew kites during significant celebrations, incuding Matariki.

ABOVE: The Carter Observatory in Wellington runs Matariki programmes. Other observatories around the country are also open to the public to observe Matariki.

> When I was in Rarotonga I was told that they used to fly kites as part of their Matariki festival. If they did I am sure Maori would have as well.
>
> *Hekenukumai Busby*

STONEHENGE AOTEAROA

It's called Stonehenge Aotearoa because
it is a blending of different cultures:
Māori, Celtic, Babylonian and so on.

LIBBY HAKARAIA

STONE CIRCLES HAVE been found throughout Europe and across Asia and the Pacific. They were the first calculators, and people used stone circles as calendars to foretell the passing of the seasons and for everyday activities such as navigation.

For those wanting to experience how the ancient world observed the rising of Matariki, Stonehenge Aotearoa in the Wairarapa will be the place to go. The project is being developed at Ahiaruhe (Carterton) by the Phoenix Astronomical Society, and is due to open at the dawn rising of Matariki in 2004.

Visitors to Stonehenge Aotearoa will be able to relearn the basic knowledge that people used thousands of years ago. As Richard Hall says:

> It's called Stonehenge Aotearoa because it is a blending of different cultures: Māori, Celtic, Babylonian and so on, and it's bringing together that knowledge that was there 10,000 years ago. The stone circles in many respects are exactly the same as a meeting house. When they talk about the posts of the house they are all to do with the solstices and the equinoxes, so

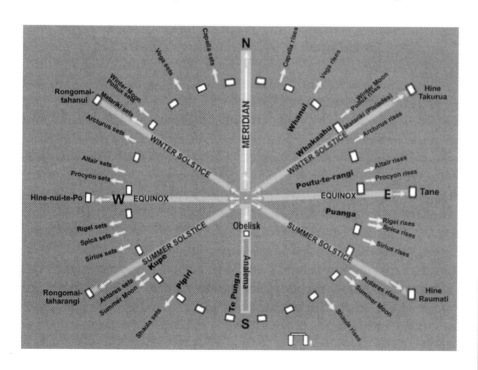

OPPOSITE PAGE:
Stonehenge Aotearoa: artist's impression of the henge onsite in the Wairarapa.
Richard Hall and Kay Leather

LEFT: The layout and names of stones at Stonehenge Aotearoa.
Richard Hall and Kay Leather

if you look at the stonehenges they are just like the posts in a meeting house and they mimic the great house in the sky, Ranginui.

Kay Leather says that, as an astronomer, her involvement in building Aotearoa Stonehenge has reminded her of why she became interested in the science in the first place.

> You like to think that you are an . . . advanced modern being but we had to check the sightings of Stonehenge and we had an equinox come up after all of the sites had been measured by a surveyor. And the way to check is to put a stick in the ground and see if the sun comes up over it — it's either right or it's wrong. The first [ray] of light appeared and there it was on the top of the stick.
>
> We are our ancestors. We like to think that we have evolved but we are still the same. I mean when we watch an eclipse we still get goosebumps. We are scientists but it moves us. I think that at Stonehenge when we have the Pleiades coming up it will give us goosebumps. It doesn't matter what culture you are, people still react in the same way.

Stonehenge Aotearoa looks similar to the famed Stonehenge ruins on the Salisbury Plains in England. However, the sizes of the stones have been adapted to the New Zealand horizon and the structure has been precisely designed and built for its location. Twenty-four monoliths, capped with lintels and rising 3 metres above the ground, stand in a circle 30 metres in diameter. At the centre of the stone circle are two larger obelisks, a sundial, a meridian line and a solar and Zodiac calendar. Four causeways lined with more stones mark the solstices and equinoxes. These extend from the centre of the circle, slicing through it and beyond the perimeter. Looking at the henge stones from the central obelisk you will be able to observe the daily rising and setting positions of the sun, moon and bright stars.

The stones are also positioned to form a Polynesian star compass. This compass marks the bearings taken by Polynesian voyagers on their travels to and from Aotearoa. Other pillars are placed and named according to the positions of seasonal stars important in Māori astronomy and cosmology, like Matariki and Whānui (Vega).

LIBBY HAKARAIA

TAINUI AND MATARIKI

MATARIKI APPEARS ON a number of flags and other adornments belonging to the monarchs of the Tainui tribe.

The descendants of the *Tainui* waka instigated the King movement or Te Kīngitanga after the Waikato land wars of the 1860s resulted in the Government confiscating vast areas of their lands. In 1894 King Mahuta became the third Māori king. His flag includes the seven stars of Matariki.

Te Paki o Matariki is the name of the flag of the Māori Queen, Te Arikinui Dame Te Atairangikaahu. It is flown at Tūrangawaewae Marae, which stands on the banks of the Waikato River in Ngāruawāhia. Te Paki o Matariki means the fine weather of Matariki and was an expression used in summer months.

Matariki also features on the doors of the wharenui, Mahinarangi, at Tūrangaewaewae.

LEFT: King Mahuta's flag incorporating the seven stars of Matariki. *Auckland War Memorial Museum Te Papa Whakahiku*

VICKI'S STORY

VICKI HYDE (TAINUI) is a science writer and author of *Night Skies Above New Zealand*. In June 1999, Vicki was asked to speak at the Tainui New Year celebrations, as a guest of the Māori Queen, Dame Te Arikinui Te Atairangikaahu, to talk about Māori astronomy. It was dark, cold and raining when the group of about 100 people crossed State Highway 1, just north of Ngāruawāhia, to stand just outside the urupā on Taupiri Mountain.

ABOVE: Vicki Hyde, who sees Matariki as a chance for all cultures to pause and reflect on those who have sailed the seas before us and those who are to come.

Just as the karakia began the clouds parted and there were the stars. Rehua was shining, a beacon of summer for our ancestors. As the night wore on we saw the *Tainui* waka in the stars, complete with triangular sail and anchor point. Non-Māori see the same stars and talk of Orion, the Hades and the Southern Cross.

Today I have learned that there are traditions that see the Southern Cross as providing a gateway to the void where the spirits go beyond death. If you find a dark sky, like that above Taupiri Mountain, you will see that void there, a vast patch of dark dust set amongst the background sparkle of unlimited stars. Early Europeans venturing into southern waters for the first time called it the Coal Sack.

One bright, bright star in the south is a personal favourite, Canopus. From my European ancestry, I know that it was seen in the constellation of Carina, the keel of the ship in Argo Navis. And it seems fitting that, from my Māori ancestry, I know that Atutahi was revered as an important guiding star for those early travellers across the seas.

This very night marks the turning of the year for Tainui, marked by the rising in the early morning of Matariki, the group of maidens, the stars which flutter on the flag outside. It is the ending of the old year, when we remember those whom we have lost, and the beginning of the new, when we look to the future.

TE PAKI O MATARIKI

Tainui orators made the following speech as they travelled around the country raising money for the building of the wharenui, Turongo, at Tūrangawaewae in the 1930s.

> *Tēnā koutou e ngā iwi e noho mai nā i ngā marae o Aituā*
> *Tēnei ahau te Paki o Matariki*
> *Te haere atu nei ki runga ki ō koutou marae*
> *He inoi ki a koutou kia āwhinatia mai te whare o ta koutou*
>   *mokopuna tamaiti*
> *E whakaarahia nei ki te tūrangawaewae o ana tūpuna mātua*

Greetings to the people who stay here at the marae of Aitua.
I, the Paki o Matariki, have come to your marae
To urge you to help the house of your grandson (King Koroki)
Be erected at the tūrangawaewae of his parents.

RIGHT: Carved wooden doors displaying the coat of arms for the Māori kings (Te Paki o Matariki) at the meeting house, Te Mahinarangi, Tūrangawaewae Marae, Ngāruawāhia.
John Houston Collection, Alexander Turnbull Library.

LIBBY HAKARAIA

WAIKATO TANIWHA RAU

Hui e tāiki e kia ora rā.
Waikato taniwha rau
He piko he taniwha
Te maunga tapu o ngā kīngi
Taupiri kia ora rā
Tūrangawaewae te marae
Tainui te waka ē
Ka mihi tātou ki te mana ki a koe
Te Ariki nui, kia kaha rā
Piki mai kake mai rā
Ngā mana o Aotearoa
Ka tū nei te ihi te wehi o
ō tātou tīpuna ē
Horahia rā tō aroha ki tō tātou taonga nei
Hui e tāiki e kia ora rā
Whakatika te piu o te poi ē
Whiua ki runga
Ki ngā tahataha
Ko Matariki e karangatia ake nei
Nau mai rā haere mai E te iwi ē.

Waikato of many chiefs
Whose sacred mountain is Taupiri
Whose marae is Tūrangawaewae
Whose ancestral canoe is *Tainui*
Greetings to Te Atairangikaahu
Greetings to the people of New Zealand.
The respect and awe of our ancestors is here today.
Embrace our Queen with love
We strive for excellence by demonstrating
     the graceful movements of poi.
Matariki is extending a warm welcome to you all today.

This famous Tainui waiata is sung at all formal occasions at Tūrangawaewae.

THE RISING OF MATARIKI

Mā te whetūrangi o Matariki, e tiaki mai, e manaaki mai i a koe,
I a koutou rānei, mō te tau e taka mai ana.

May the gentle light of Matariki guide and inspire you all this year.

FESTIVALS MARKING MATARIKI, the traditional Māori New Year, are fast gaining acceptance and recognition as a time of celebration most uniquely relevant to Aotearoa New Zealand.

Matariki is linked to the universal celebration of midwinter. It's the antipodean equivalent of the Scots' Hogmanay or the Chinese New Year — in fact, it has traditions that go back further than the Roman Saturnalia. Given such antecedents, it is perhaps not surprising that, after 150 years of European settlement, there is a move to return to the natural order of things and to synchronise midwinter celebrations with — midwinter! Whether it's acknowledged by a dip in the sea or a feast or a solstice dinner (and certainly all these seem more common now than in the past) or merely by noting the 'shortest day', there seems to be a universal need to recognise 'the darkest hour' when the sun has reached its lowest point, so that we can look forward to its return. For our geographical location, the rising of Matariki is the signal that the solstice is on its way, so Matariki is one Māori tradition which non-Māori can both relate to and celebrate.

Marilyn Head, editor of Galaxy Magazine

LIBBY HAKARAIA

MATARIKI POEM

Matariki turns
her face to us once more
it's a wonder she returns
year after year
when so many celebrate
the beginning of the year
on the 1st of January
with wine and beer

Auē te wareware
ki a koutou e
ngā whetū o runga
te whenua o raro
whakahokia
wairua mai
kia mahara tātau
ki a koutou e

Matariki turns
her face to us once more
this year
again
we will remember her
with ritual
hāngī
dance
and song
by telling her the names
of all of those who've gone

Haere koutou
ki tōna pae
ko te paepae o Matariki
mai i reira ai
whakahokia
wairua mai
kia mahara tātau
ki a koutou e

Jacq Carter

APPENDIX — MAORI NAMES FOR STARS, MONTHS, SEASONS ETC

MILKY WAY AND NEBULAE

Kapua Puehu o Tautoru	The Orion Nebula (M42)
Matanuku	Large Magellanic Cloud
Ngā Pātari	Magellanic Clouds
Ngā Pātari Kaihau	Small Magellanic Cloud
Te Ikaroa/Te Māngōroa	The Milky Way
Te Pātiki	The Coal Sack

SUN, MOON AND PLANETS

Rā	Sun
Marama	Moon
Whiro	Mercury
Kōpū	Venus
Papatūānuku	Earth
Matawhero	Mars
Kōpūnui	Jupiter
Pareārau	Saturn
Rangipō	Uranus
Tangaroa	Neptune
Whiringa ki Tawhiti	Pluto

LIBBY HAKARAIA

STARS AND CONSTELLATIONS

Autahi/Atutahi	Canopus
Kaikōpere	Sagittarius
Māhutonga	Southern Cross
Mairerangi	Scorpio (body)
Marere-o-tonga	Archernar
Matamata Kāheru	Hyades
Matariki	Pleiades
Ō-tama-rākau	Fomalhaut
Pāwai	The False Cross
Poutū-te-Rangi	Altair
Puangahori	Procyon
Puanga	Rigel
Pukawanui	Canis Major (triangle)
Pūtara	Betelgeuse
Ranginui	Beta Centauri (closest pointer)
Rehua	Antares
Ruawāhia	Arcturus
Takurua	Sirius
Tama-rereti	Scorpio (tail)
Taumata-kuku	Aldebaran
Tautoru	Orion's Belt
Uruao	Alpha Centauri (furthest pointer)
Whakaahu kerekere	Pollux
Whakaahu rangi	Castor
Whānui	Vega
Whetū Kaipō	Bellatrix
Whetū Matarau	The Pointers (to the Southern Cross)
Whiti-kaupeka	Spica

MONTHS OF THE YEAR

01	Pipiri	June
02	Hongonui	July
03	Here-turi-kōkā	August
04	Mahuru	September
05	Whiringa-ā-nuku	October
06	Whiringa-ā-rangi	November
07	Hakihea	December
08	Kohitātea	January
09	Hui-tanguru	February
10	Poutūterangi	March
11	Paenga-whāwhā	April
12	Haratua	May

SEASONS

Takurua/Hōtoke   Winter
Takurua is the name commonly given to the star Sirius. The personified name Hine-takura which means the winter maiden.
Hōtoke means cold.

Kōanga/Mahuru   Spring
Kōanga is the planting time; kō means to dig or plant.
Mahuru is the personified form of spring.

Raumati   Summer
Raumati is personified as the being Hine-raumati. One legend has Hine-raumati mating with Raro, the underworld. Their offspring were Matariki, Puanga and Takurua.

Ngahuru   Autumn
Ngahuru means 10 and therefore denotes the tenth month in the Māori calendar. This is the time of crop lifting, when food was plentiful.

BIBLIOGRAPHY

Batten, Juliet, *Celebrating the Southern Seasons*, Tandem Press, Auckland 1995.

Best, Elsdon, *The Astronomical Knowledge of the Maori*. Government Print, Wellington, 1922.

— *Forest Lore of the Maori*, Government Print, Wellington, 1922.

— *Maori Agriculture*, Government Print, Wellington, 1922.

— *Polynesian Voyages; The Maori as a Deep-Sea Navigator, Explorer and Colonizer*. Government Print, Wellington, 1922.

Dansey, Harry, in *Te Ao Hou*, vol. 16, 1967–68.

Hilder, CJ, 'Māori Star and Constellation Names', compiled June 2000–May 2003, www.teapot.orcon.net.nz/maori_star_names.html.

Hyde, Vicki, *Night Skies Above New Zealand*, New Holland, Auckland, 2003.

Mead, Hirini Moko & Grove, Neil, *Nga Pepeha a nga Tipuna*, Victoria University Press, Wellington, 2001.

Ngata, AT & Pei Te Hurinui Jones, *Nga Moteatea*, Part 3, The Polynesian Society, 1980.

Orbell, Margaret, *The Illustrated Encyclopaedia of Māori Myth and Legend*, Canterbury University Press, Christchurch, 1995.

Te Taura Whiri i te Reo Māori (Māori Language Commission), 'Matariki: Te Whetu o te Tau' (booklet).

White, John, *The Ancient History of the Maori*, 6 vols, Government Printer, Wellington, 1887–90.